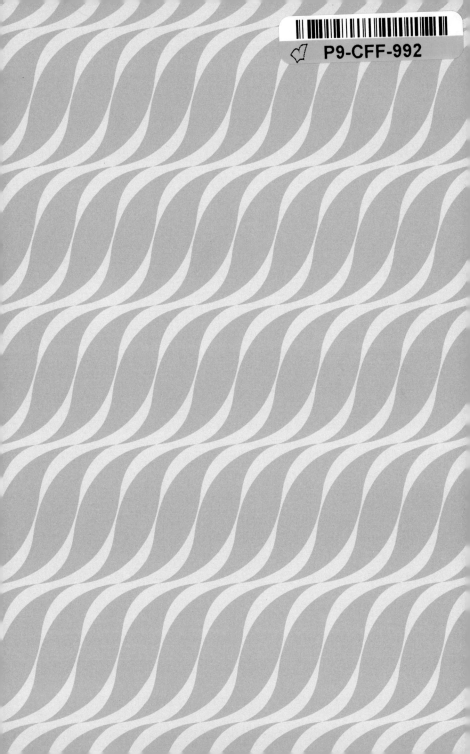

THE NEW PLANT LIBRARY

FOLIAGE COLOR

THE NEW PLANT LIBRARY

FOLIAGE
COLOR

BRYAN GREENWOOD

Consultant: Andrew Mikolajski
Photography by Andrea Jones

southwater

To Jane Lister, with thanks for all her help

This edition is published by Southwater

Distributed in the UK by The Manning Partnership
251–253 London Road East
Batheaston, Bath BA1 7RL
tel. 01225 852 727 fax 01225 852 852

Distributed in Canada by General Publishing
895 Don Mills Road, 400–402 Park Centre
Toronto, Ontario M3C 1W3
tel. 416 445 3333 fax 416 445 5991

Published in the USA by Anness Publishing Inc.
27 West 20th Street, Suite 504
New York, NY 10011
fax 212 807 6813

Distributed in Australia by Sandstone Publishing
Unit 1, 360 Norton Street, Leichhardt
New South Wales 2040
tel. 02 9560 7888 fax 02 9560 7488

Southwater is an imprint of Anness Publishing Limited
Hermes House, 88–89 Blackfriars Road, London SE1 8HA
tel. 020 7401 2077; fax 020 7633 9499

© Anness Publishing Limited 2001

Publisher Joanna Lorenz
Managing Editor Judith Simons
Editors Martin Goldring and Polly Willis
Designer Michael Morey
Photographer Andrea Jones
Production Controller Joanna King

Previously published in a larger format

Printed and bound in China

1 3 5 7 9 10 8 6 4 2

■ HALF TITLE PAGE
Lobelia cardinalis
■ FRONTISPIECE
The great variety of coloured foliage
■ TITLE PAGE
Heuchera 'Stormy Seas'

■ LEFT
Helichrysum italicum
■ OPPOSITE LEFT
Acer palmatum
■ OPPOSITE RIGHT
Heuchera 'Pewter Moon'

Contents

*T*he last 20 years have seen a quiet but notice-able growth in the popularity of coloured foliage in gardens. It is now possible to obtain all types of plants including trees, shrubs, climbers and perennials that boast a range of colours all the way from the palest of greys through yellow, orange, bronze, red and purple to black. In theory, at least, it is possible to create a garden without ever using the colour green, though in practice the beauty of coloured foliage is the way that it combines so well with more conventional plants.

Combining background information, an essential grower's guide and an extensive catalogue of plants, this practical guide to coloured foliage will help you to create stunning oases of colour in your garden that will give you pleasure throughout the year.

■ RIGHT
While the orange flowers of these *Canna* hybrids link them to the other plants, the burgundy foliage gives a dramatic contrast.

Why do plants have coloured foliage?

Fundamentally, all leaves are green. The green pigment is chlorophyll, a substance present in all leaves, which allows plants to absorb energy from sunlight and convert it into sugars for growth. Without chlorophyll, plants would die.

Plant leaves also contain other pigments: xanthophyll is yellow, carotene orange-red and anthocyamin red and purple. In nearly all cases, the chlorophyll predominates and masks out the other colours, but in some cases one or more of the other colours prevails, though this effect can be temporary.

For instance, some plants (notably *Pieris*, *Photinia* and some maples) produce a flush of red leaves in spring which by summer have turned green as more chlorophyll is produced to help the plant absorb sunlight. Yellow-leaved plants tend to become progressively greener as the season advances. In autumn, the reverse effect can be observed in many deciduous trees and shrubs and some perennials. The chlorophyll begins to break down as the days shorten, and the other colours briefly become apparent before the leaves drop.

Some plants, however retain a leaf colour other than green throughout most of the growing season, but

■ ABOVE
The striking silvery leaves of *Helichrysum italicum* ssp. *serotinum* have a distinctive aroma and can be used in cooking.

■ BELOW
Euonymus alatus is a deciduous shrub whose dark green leaves turn bright scarlet in autumn.

exactly why and how is not entirely understood. In some cases, red-purple overlays the green, giving a bronze tinge to the leaves.

Grey and silver leaves arise as a response to certain climatic conditions, usually to help protect the leaf from excessive moisture loss during periods of prolonged drought. Some leaves appear to be covered in a fine white powder (and are botanically described as pruinose) or a mealy substance (farinose), giving a suede-like appearance. Others have a waxy bloom that makes the leaves appear bluish green or bluish grey (sometimes almost white), a colour that is often defined as "glaucous" (a term classically used of the sea). If any of these are rubbed off, the true green of the leaf can be seen underneath.

Sometimes the leaves also have a reduced surface area and are chubby, to retain moisture - these are known as succulents, familiar examples being *Sedum* and *Sempervivum*. (The most extreme examples of this phenomenon are cacti, outside the scope of this book.)

Some plants have leaves that are covered in hair to prevent excess evaporation of moisture from the leaf surface, as in the case of bunny's ears (*Stachys byzantina*), making them

■ BELOW
A well-designed bed containing nothing
but foliage plants can look every bit as
striking as a display of flowers.

appear silvery grey. Leaves of *Ballota pseudodictamnus* and *Buddleja crispa* appear "felted" or woolly.

Variegation – where chlorophyll is absent from parts of the leaf, which are thus white, cream, yellow or (occasionally) pink – can be due to the presence of a virus but in most cases seems to arise naturally.

It is a strange fact of gardening that once they are introduced to cultivation many plants begin to exhibit a wider range of variation than they ever do in the wild. It seems that most plants carry enormous potential in their genes but that the environment in the wild favours the survival only of green-leaved seedlings – which are always more vigorous. Coloured-leaved plants are therefore nearly all of garden origin, and the colours have been consolidated by careful selection and repeated back-crossings by nurserymen to produce the wide range of forms that are now available to gardeners.

Which plants have coloured foliage?

Coloured leaves appear in nearly all plant groups, usually as named selections (straight species normally have plain green leaves) or as man-made hybrids.

How to recognize coloured leaf forms

Plant names are often descriptive, and the leaf colour may be immediately evident, as in *Heuchera micrantha* var. *diversifolia* 'Palace Purple' or *Phormium* 'Bronze Baby'. Latin cultivar names often indicate leaf colour, 'Glauca' signifying blue-grey leaves, 'Argentea' silver and 'Aurea' yellow or gold. Purple or red leaves can be signalled by 'Atropurpurea' (or

■ ABOVE
Ophiopogon planiscapus 'Nigrescens', the name of which alludes to the black foliage.

■ BELOW
Here, *Pittosporum tenuifolium* sets off the aptly-named *Choisya ternata* 'Sundance'.

'Purpurea') or 'Rubra'. Plants with variegated leaves are often known as 'Argenteovariegata' or 'Aureovariegata' (depending on whether the variegation is white or yellow), sometimes as just 'Variegata' (or 'Marginata' – "margined"). 'Maculata' indicates a splashing of the leaves, as in *Elaeagnus pungens* 'Maculata'.

Sometimes, however, particularly where there are many varieties, as in the case of hostas, the name provides no clue whatsoever. While the hostas 'Blue Angel' and 'Piedmont Gold' are self-evidently blue and yellow respectively, 'Krossa Regal' and 'Love Pat' are also glaucous, while 'Sum and Substance' and 'Zounds' are old gold.

Conifers

For year-round leaf colour, conifers are unmatched. Top of the list is the Blue Atlas cedar, *Cedrus atlantica* f. *glauca*, with leaves that are a bright glaucous blue. 'Aurea' has golden yellow new leaves that age green. Dwarf conifers include *Picea pungens* 'Globosa' (blue) and *Thuja plicata* 'Aurea Nana', a golden egg at 60cm (24in) high. Note that golden yellow conifers have their best leaf colour in spring (on the new growth), while blue-leaved varieties develop their

■ BELOW
This *Thuja plicata* 'Irish Gold' will have its
most impressive leaf colour in spring.

most intense colour after a cold spell
in winter.

Trees and shrubs

Coloured-leaved plants in this
category tend to be deciduous, but
there are a few exceptions, notably
Eucalyptus gunnii, a versatile plant
which can be grown as a tree or a
shrub, with shining silver-blue leaves,
and *Pittosporum*, a genus of shrubs
that contains many purple-leaved and
variegated varieties. There are many
hebes with purple or silver leaves.
Heathers offer exciting possibilities,
some having cream or pink young
shoot tips in spring, others turning
red or orange as the temperature dips
in winter.

A notable deciduous tree is the
golden-leaved form of the Indian
bean tree, *Catalpa bignonioides*
'Aurea', with large, heart-shaped
leaves, but the widest range of
possibilities is to be found among the
maples, with a huge number of cultivars with rich red-purple or golden-
yellow leaves. Some are excitingly
variegated with cream and pink.

Sub-shrubs (an intermediate
category with firmer stems than a
perennial but with a tendency to die
back) include many of the

Mediterranean plants with grey
leaves: sage (*Salvia*), lavender
(*Lavandula*) and the woolly-leaved
Ballota pseudodictamnus. There are
many shrubby artemisias, some with
almost whitened leaves.

Perennials

Perennials offer the gardener plenty
of scope. Queen of all foliage plants is
the hosta, with a huge range of
cultivars with both glaucous and
golden-yellow leaves. There are also
some variegated varietes, such as
'Frances Williams', with thick blue

leaves edged with beige-cream, and,
most dramatic of all, *H. flucutans*
'Sagae', with huge sea-green leaves
margined with creamy yellow.

Purple-leaved perennials include
Lobelia cardinalis 'Victoria', a strong
feature even before the clashing
scarlet flowers appear, and
Ophiopogon planiscapus 'Nigrescens',
a grassy plant whose leaves appear
almost black.

Grey-leaved perennials include
Stachys byzantina, indispensable in
any garden; the cultivar 'Silver
Carpet' is non-flowering. There are
also a number of useful "blue"
grasses: *Festuca glauca* 'Blaufuchs' and
Leymus arenarius 'Glaucus'.

Annuals

Most annuals are grown for their
flowers, but there are a few that are
grown for their leaves, all making
useful infillers in a border. *Senecio
cineraria* 'Silver Dust' is, as its name
suggests, a grey-leaved plant that is
widely used in park bedding schemes.
Among the most exciting of all
foliage plants is coleus (*Solenostemon
scutellarioides*); various strains have
highly patterned leaves in shades of
red, yellow, purple, brown and
creamy white.

Using coloured foliage in the garden

■ BELOW
The blackish-purple leaves of *Pittosporum tenuifolium* 'Purpureum' look stunning when combined with brighter colours.

Foliage can have as much impact in the garden as flowers. From the design point of view, the advantage of plants with coloured leaves is that their presence is felt for much longer than that of most flowering plants, whose season of interest is comparatively brief. Remember, however, that some plants that are grown mainly for their flowers also have striking foliage that can be exploited as an integral part of the design. Many peonies have sumptuous, glossy bronze-purple leaves, for instance, and carnations have blue-grey leaves of very long-lasting appeal.

Most plants with coloured foliage have very specific cultivation requirements, particularly as regards how much sunlight they receive. Further, most make such a strong impact that you need to judge carefully where they will make their maximum effect without detracting from your other plants.

Yellow-leaved plants

These are often at their freshest in spring as the new growth emerges, and will light up any area of the garden. The shrubs *Philadelphus coronarius* 'Aureus' (deciduous) and *Choisya ternata* 'Sundance' (evergreen) are both equally vivid and provide a good foil to spring-flowering daffodils (either yellow or white) or, more excitingly, purple crocuses. Bowles' golden grass

■ LEFT
Choisya ternata 'Sundance' is a versatile plant that combines as well with other bright leaves as it contrasts with dark ones.

perennials, *Heuchera micrantha* var. *diversifolia* 'Palace Purple' will slowly make carpets of beetroot-red leaves in sun or shade, as will *Ajuga reptans* 'Burgundy Glow'.

Generally, the leaf colour of purple-leaved plants deepens as the season advances, though the initial sheen is often lost. By late summer, many purple-leaved plants have a sombre, almost funereal appearance.

(*Milium effusum* 'Aureum') is a good choice for filling gaps in bedding schemes.

In late spring the velvety leaves of *Catalpa bignonioides* 'Aurea' start to unfurl and will be at their best in early summer. After midsummer, most yellow-leaved plants become progressively greener.

Red- and purple-leaved plants

These include some of the most dramatic of all plants. Again, the leaf colour is most vivid in spring. The red new leaves of *Photinia* 'Red Robin' and *Pieris* 'Forest Flame' are particularly welcome then, since this is a colour unusual in flowering plants around this time. The new growth of purple-leaved Japanese maples (*Acer palmatum* cvs) has an almost metallic brilliance. Among

Grey-, silver- and blue-leaved plants

Unlike the previous two groups, these are usually at their best at the height of summer, since their leaf colour is a response to strong sunlight. The

exceptions are conifers, which have their most intense colour after a cold snap. Site these where they will be lit up by the winter sun.

Being of a neutral colour, these plants complement all others and never clash. Most are best in a sunny, open position (though all hostas prefer some shade).

■ ABOVE RIGHT
The bloodied blades of *Imperata cylindrica* 'Rubra' contrast vividly with our normal expectations of how grass looks.

■ LEFT
The purple leaves of this *Cotinus coggygria* 'Royal Purple' will turn red in the autumn.

■ BELOW
Elymus magellanicus has unusually metallic
and vibrant foliage for a blue-leaved plant.

The blue Atlas cedar is a magnificent tree that is best seen as a specimen in solitary isolation, either in a lawn or to mark a focal point. In a confined space, the deciduous weeping willow-leaved pear (*Pyrus salicifolia* 'Pendula') makes a shimmering silver curtain.

The low-growing *Stachys byzantina* is a good edging plant; if you need to fill a large area, try *Senecio viravira*, a sprawling sub-shrub with whitened stems and leaves that can even be persuaded to climb if given support.

Blue-leaved hostas are a traditional accompaniment to roses, associating well with the subtly coloured old-fashioned types in shades of pink, dusky purple and cream.

Variegated plants

These can be difficult to place, since their leaves combine two (sometimes three) colours; all tend to be very eye-catching. Variegated hollies (*Ilex*) make good specimens that provide year-round interest. Maples (varieties of *Acer japonicum* and *A. palmatum*) are good deciduous alternatives. Many shrubs have variegated cultivars, and these are often useful in a small garden, since they are always less vigorous than their plain-leaved

parents. One of the loveliest of all is *Euonymus fortunei* 'Silver Queen', particularly since the leaves have a very wide white margin; it is spectacular when trained against a wall.

It is a neat idea to pick out the colour of the variegation in nearby plants. The leaves of *Weigela florida* 'Variegata' are margined with white when young, combining well with white daffodils, this colour deepening to yellow by summer, when a gold-leaved hosta will be its friend.

Combining plants

Gardening is all about putting plants together, playing with colours, shapes and textures, and coloured-leaved

plants offer plenty of exciting possibilities.

For a "hot" scheme, try mixing purple-leaved shrubs, such as *Pittosporum tenuifolium* 'Tom Thumb' or hebes, with red-leaved annual coleus. Colours would be at their richest by late summer, when the flowers could include yellow, orange and red dahlias ('Bishop of Llandaff' has purple leaves) and annual nasturtiums in the same shades. For added drama, include a few upright plants such as cannas ('Black Knight' has bronze leaves and dark red flowers) and spiky phormiums (*P. tenax* 'Dazzler' has bronze leaves striped red, orange and pink).

You could cool down such a scheme with grey-leaved artemisias or *Stachys byzantina*, or alternatively a few well-chosen grasses in blue or beige-green. Rising above all could be the South African *Melianthus major*, a stunning sub-shrub with exotic-looking grey-green leaves, easily reaching 2m (6ft) or more in a hot summer.

Purples and bronzes can also be used in cool, sophisticated schemes. You could alternate pollarded eucalyptus with purple-leaved berberis at regular intervals in a long border to give rhythm to a mixed planting of spring-flowering bulbs followed by summer annuals. For a seasonal screen, interplant eucalyptus and *Prunus cerasifera* 'Nigra'. Cut back the eucalyptus annually before the prunus comes into flower (on the bare stems). By midsummer, you will have a solid screen banded bronze and silver, an effective backdrop for a wide range of plants.

Yellow- and purple-leaved plants also look good in combination, as they are virtually complementary; but uniting colours in the same range can be comparably striking. A sweep of yellows might include a golden-leaved conifer for height and structure, underplanted with a yellow-variegated euonymus, a hosta such as 'Sum and Substance' and the yellowish-grey *Stachys byzantina* 'Primrose Heron'. The orange-brown grass *Stipa arundinacea* could supply a deeper accent.

Finally, do not forget the value of plain green in the garden. Indiscriminate use of plants with coloured foliage can lead to a garish, unsettling scheme. This can be exciting, but to tone down (or even highlight) your wildest schemes, include a large evergreen such as a holly, camellia or *Viburnum rhytidophyllum* that will have a calming effect.

■ LEFT
(Before) A metal
trough in winter.

■ BELOW
(After) The same
trough given a
new lease of life
using coloured-
foliage plants.

Plant Catalogue

The plants within the catalogue are broadly divided into colour categories. It must however be appreciated that colour is quite subjective in that one person's purple is another person's burgundy, and in plants it is also affected by growing conditions and light. This list of coloured-leaved plants has therefore been divided as seems most suitable to us. It should really serve to whet your appetite as many more are available and new varieties are constantly being developed.

■ ABOVE RIGHT
ACAENA 'BLUE HAZE'

An evergreen ground-cover plant for places where the competing plants are not too vigorous. Its steel-blue leaflets contrast beautifully with the reddish flowerheads that it produces in the summer and that turn into dark red burrs with pinkish spines in the autumn. *Acaena* requires full or partial sun and well-drained soil to thrive. It makes a particularly successful combination with the bright orange of *Libertia perigrinans*. Height 10cm (4in), spread 30cm (12in). Perennial.

■ RIGHT
CUPRESSUS GLABRA 'BLUE ICE'

Known sometimes as the smooth cypress, this conifer has smooth, flaky bark, the warm brown colour of which is an excellent counterpoint to the spiral sprays of its striking blue-grey foliage. It requires good drainage and full sun. Though naturally a fairly tight, well-shaped conifer, its height and width can be controlled by light trimming with shears. Height 10.5m (35ft), spread 4.5m (15ft). Tree.

Blues

■ ABOVE
ELYMUS MAGELLANICUS

An unusual evergreen grass valued for its distinctive, metallic, blue foliage. It is tolerant of relatively dry conditions, but does require full sun. *Elymus hispiculus*, better known as blue wheat grass, forms bright, upright clumps that are neater than those of *Elymus magellanicus*. It also produces narrow green and white flower spikes in summer. Height 30cm (12in), spread 45cm (18in). Grass.

■ ABOVE RIGHT
FESTUCA GLAUCA

Blue fescue grass is one of a genus of 80 or so species of hardy perennial ornamental grasses. They require light well-drained soil in full sun and can be used for edging or making an interesting contrast when mixed with heathers. This plant has oval pale purple spikelets that appear in summer. Height 25cm (9in), spread 30cm (12in). Grass.

■ ABOVE
HOSTA 'BLUE WEDGWOOD'

This beautiful hosta is a member of the Tardiana Group. It is slow to show its mature habit but it is worth waiting for. Its blue heart-shaped leaves and lavender-coloured flowers are a sight to behold. Mulch in autumn and spring – a dark brown mulch such as composted bark will beautifully set off the emerging leaves which are one of the joys of the spring border. Height and spread 90cm (3ft). Perennial.

■ ABOVE
HOSTA 'HADSPEN BLUE'

One of the smaller hostas, and also in the Tardiana Group, the
heart-shaped grey-blue leaves of this delightful plant are enhanced
by pale lavender-coloured flowers. It prefers light shade, in moist
soil that is well fertilized and mulched annually. Height 30cm
(12in), spread 30cm (12in). Perennial.

■ RIGHT
HOSTA 'HALCYON'

Another member of the Tardiana group, this is a graceful plant
with bright silver-grey leaves and heavy clusters of smoky-lilac
flowers that appear in late summer. Not to be planted in shade if
the full colour of the foliage is to be enjoyed but does benefit from
moist soil. Can be propagated by dividing in autumn or spring.
Height 45cm (18in), spread 50cm (20in). Perennial.

■ ABOVE
JUNIPERUS SQUAMATA 'BLUE STAR' AGM

This is a good plant to use for ground cover if planted in sufficient numbers. Once it is established, its low-growing habit and spreading branches will help to suppress weeds and retain moisture. It provides dense and relatively small rounded areas of blue, and thus is easy to contrast strategically with other colours in a flowerbed. Plant in full sun. Height 50cm (20in), spread 60cm (24in). Tree.

■ ABOVE
PICEA PUNGENS 'HOOPSII' AGM

Has one of the best blues that can be found, and it is particularly striking when contrasted with dark green foliage of other plants. *Picea pungens* is an open-branched tree of conical shape with prickly, stiff needles radiating from stout shoots and scaly grey bark. There is also a weeping form (with low-hanging branches), *Picea pungens* 'Glauca Pendula', but it does not have the same captivating blue as 'Hoopsii'. Height 7.5m (25ft), spread 3m (10ft). Tree.

■ RIGHT
RUTA GRAVEOLENS
'JACKMAN'S BLUE' AGM

Better known as rue, *Ruta graveolens* is traditionally regarded as a symbol of repentance by virtue of this common name. Its strongly-scented (not to everyone's taste), bitter-tasting leaves were formerly used in medicine, but this useful compact evergreen is now prized for its fern-like blue foliage and the clusters of yellow flowers that appear in summer. It requires full sun and well-drained soil for best results. Height 60cm (24in), spread 75cm (30in). Shrub.

Yellows and golds

■ LEFT
ACORUS GRAMINEUS
'VARIEGATUS'

Marginal water plant of garden origin,
though the species comes originally from
China and Japan. This variegated variety
tends to be a little less hardy than the all-
green form, but its grasslike leaves have
creamy white margins and help to provide
pockets of interest around the pond in
winter. It does well in wet soil or covered
with up to 10cm (4in) of water. Grow in
full sun and divide congested clumps in
spring. Height 25cm (10in), spread 15cm
(6in). Perennial.

■ LEFT
CALLUNA VULGARIS 'ARRAN
GOLD'

Heather with racemes of purple flowers
from midsummer to late autumn and
bright golden-yellow foliage that is lime-
green flecked with red in winter. Keep it
happy by growing it in acid soil and
keeping well mulched with peat or any
lime-free substitute. Height 15cm (6in),
spread 25cm (10in). Shrub.

■ ABOVE
CHOISYA TERNATA
'SUNDANCE' AGM

This popular yellow shrub is evergreen, rounded and dense with glossy bright yellow leaves. Clusters of white star-shaped flowers appear in the late spring and frequently in the autumn. It is unfussy about soil as long as it is well drained. Shade, though, will often make the foliage turn green, while some few individuals will bleach in full sun. Height 1.5m (5ft), spread 1.2m (4ft). Shrub.

■ ABOVE
CAREX ELATA 'AUREA' (SYN. *C. STRICTA* 'AUREA')

Marginal water plant of garden origin grown for its bright golden-yellow leaves. Its bright colour makes it a good focal point and it contrasts well with burgundy-leaved plants. Grow in full sun and divide congested clumps in spring. Height to 40cm (16in), spread 60cm (24in). Sedge.

■ RIGHT
CORNUS ALBA 'AUREA' AGM

As well as its yellow foliage, this deciduous shrub has the bonus of bright red stems that show beautifully in the winter. To take full advantage of this, plant where the light conditions will make them look their best, say against a dark background or positioned to catch the setting sun, and prune to 5–8cm (2–3in) above the ground every other spring. *Cornus alba* 'Aurea' does best on moist soil. Height 1.8m (6ft), spread 1.5m (5ft). Shrub.

■ ABOVE
CORTADERIA SELLOANA 'GOLD BAND' AGM

An elegant variety of pampas grass that is native to South America. Pampas grass can be found growing wild in abundance on the plains south of the Amazon, but its simple, elegant appearance makes 'Gold Band' an excellent ornamental plant for use in the garden. It has leaves that grow progressively more yellow as the year continues and plumes that can reach 1.5–1.8m (5–6ft) tall. *Cortaderia selloana* 'Gold Band' is an evergreen that grows best in an open position in well-drained soil. Height 1.2m (4ft), spread 1.5m (5ft). Grass.

■ ABOVE RIGHT
ERICA CINEREA 'FIDDLER'S GOLD'

A heather that boasts urn-shaped, lilac-pink flowers from early summer to early autumn and spectacular bright golden-yellow foliage that turns red in winter. This is a compact plant that prefers a warm, dry position, and it should be planted in an acid soil and kept well watered until established. It should be mulched annually with either peat or a lime-free peat substitute. *Erica cinerea* 'Fiddler's Gold' produces its best leaf colour in spring. Height 25cm (10in), spread 45cm (18in). Shrub.

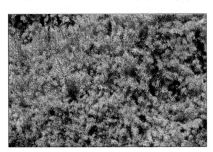

■ ABOVE
ERICA CINEREA 'GOLDEN DROP'

Heather with bright golden-yellow foliage that is tinged copper on emergence in spring and turns copper-red in winter. The sparse, urn-shaped, lilac-pink flowers, produced from early summer to early autumn, are best removed. *Erica cinerea* 'Golden Drop' has a prostrate, mat-like habit that is good for ground cover. Height 20cm (8in), spread 60cm (24in). Shrub.

■ BELOW
ERICA VAGANS 'VALERIE PROUDLEY'

Heather with cylindrical to bell-shaped, sparse, white flowers from
midsummer to mid-autumn and bright lemon-yellow leaves. The
foliage of *Erica vagans* 'Valerie Proudley' is of good colour
throughout the year and it is a very good heather for a container.
Height 15cm (6in), spread 30cm (12in). Shrub.

■ ABOVE
EUONYMOUS JAPONICUS 'OVATUS AUREUS'

A compact slow-growing shrub that needs a sunny site to retain its
stunning yellow oval-shaped leaves. Being evergreen it is a useful
plant in many different types of schemes, even as a hedge, and
provides year-round colour and interest, especially in winter when
the leaves will brighten the dullest of days. It grows to a height and
spread of 1m (3ft) in 3 years and eventually to 3m (10ft). Plant in
any type of good garden soil. Shrub.

■ ABOVE
HEDERA HELIX 'BUTTERCUP' AGM

A vigorous evergreen climber, this ivy is conspicuous for its lovely
rich yellow leaves which turn to a pale green as they age. It grows
well against walls, trees or fences in any good soil. The leaf colour is
at its best in a good light. Trim it lightly when it becomes untidy.
When planting against a house wall, plant 45cm (18in) from the base
of the wall where the soil will be better and it will be out of the rain
shadow caused by the eaves. Add plenty of organic matter, and water
well until established. Height and spread indefinite. Climber.

■ ABOVE
HEDERA HELIX 'JERSEY DORIS'

This ivy from the island of Jersey, United Kingdom, has typical ivy
leaves with five broad lobes as wide as they are long. New growth is
creamy white with pretty speckles and blotches of green, sometimes
becoming mottled, the old leaves are green all over. Grow in good
light for best results. Best suited for a border or up a wall. Height
and spread indefinite. Climber.

■ ABOVE RIGHT
JASMINIUM OFFICINALE 'FIONA SUNRISE'

A relatively new introduction, this deciduous climber has all the
attributes of the ordinary green-leaved jasmine i.e. vigorous growth
and sweetly scented flowers, as well as golden-yellow foliage.
Scrambling over a sheltered archway or pergola is the best way to
fully appreciate the scent but it does equally well on an east, west or
south facing wall. No pruning is necessary and it thrives in any
fertilized, well-drained soil, but keep well watered if planted at the
base of a wall. Height 4m (13ft), spread 3m (10ft). Climber.

■ RIGHT
MILIUM EFFUSUM 'AUREUM'

This tuft-forming, perennial, evergreen grass has attractive golden
leaves and produces branched flowerheads of greenish-yellow
spikelets in the summer. It is a particularly useful grass because it
retains its colour even in shade. *Milium effusum* 'Aureum' prefers
moist conditions, so incorporate plenty of organic material into the
ground, keep it well watered and mulch regularly. Height 40cm
(16in), spread 40cm (16in). Grass.

■ ABOVE
TAXUS BACCATA
'ELEGANTISSIMA' AGM

Although this slow-growing yew is capable
of eventually becoming a small tree, like all
yews it can be trimmed to the desired
shape and size, and is therefore an ideal
candidate for topiary. Its attractive foliage
and its convenient tolerance for a wide
range of growing conditions make this
evergreen an excellent choice. Height 4.5m
(15ft), spread 4.5m (15ft). Tree.

■ RIGHT
THUJA PLICATA 'IRISH GOLD'

Usually a dwarf conifer, as a selection of a
much larger species from North America.
It forms a conical shrub. The scale-like
leaves are bright yellow-green with lighter
patches; the cones are green initially,
maturing to brown. 'Irish Gold' is one of
the most decorative selections of *Thuja
plicata*. Height and spread generally to 2m
(6.5ft), though it can eventually reach a
height of 20m (66ft) or more. Tree.

Oranges and browns

■ ABOVE
ASTILBE

■ ABOVE
CALLUNA VULGARIS 'BLAZEAWAY'

The beautiful filigree leaves of astilbes provide a light and delicate backdrop for the feather-like flowers that appear in summer. Essentially a bog plant, they grow well with some types of iris as well as hostas, where the different types of foliage provide a fine contrast. They grow best in full sun or light shade, but the soil must be moist and rich. Height from 15cm (6in) to 60cm (24in), spread from 10cm (4in) to 1m (3ft). Perennial.

As the year goes on the colour of this heather gradually progresses to a deeper orange, until late summer when the arrival of flowers changes it yet again. One of the larger heathers, it mixes well with birch trees, especially multi-stemmed *Betula utilis* var. *jacquemontii*, as well as azaleas and small rhododendrons. Plant in large groups for the best colour effect. Always avoid soil containing lime or chalk and plant in an open aspect. Keep well watered until established. Height 45cm (18in), spread 55cm (22in). Shrub.

■ RIGHT
CAREX BUCHANANII

An elegant, arching, clump-forming
evergreen grass with narrow copper-
coloured leaves (red towards the base) that
turn more towards orange in the winter. *C.
buchananii* blends well with other bronze-
or copper-coloured plants and is a good
contrast to blues and greys. Requires
moisture-retentive soil and looks its best in
full sun. Height 75cm (30in), spread 45cm
(18in). Grass.

■ ABOVE
CALLUNA VULGARIS 'SPITFIRE'

Heathers have a wide range of foliage colour
from pale lemon to rich orange. This one
also has mauve flowers from later summer
onwards. It is ideal for rock gardens and
ground cover and a good foil for some of the
smaller ornamental grasses. Dwarf conifers
also make popular planting companions.
Plant in acid soil in an open, well-drained
site, first applying a 5cm (2in) layer of
ericaceous compost. Water well in dry
weather and dress soil with ericaceous
compost each spring. Height 25cm (10in),
spread 40cm (16in). Shrub.

■ ABOVE AND INSET LEFT
CRYPTOMERIA JAPONICA 'TEN SAN'

A tightly-formed little ball-like conifer that looks a bit like a sponge from a
distance. Its foliage has a beautiful warm russet-brown colour and because it is
also so small and slow-growing, it is a useful component in schemes involving
alpines and some of the less vigorous heathers. It requires full sun and a light
soil and does not take kindly to trimming. Height 45cm (18in), spread 30cm
(12in). Tree.

■ LEFT
FOENICULUM VULGARE 'PURPUREUM'

This where colour becomes subjective. Although it has "purpureum" in the title many would say this form of the herb fennel is more brown than purple. Either way, its delicate filigree foliage is an asset to any border. Plant in full sun, in friable soil and keep well watered until established. Height 1.5m (5ft), spread 0.6m (2ft). Perennial.

■ ABOVE
MAGNOLIA GRANDIFLORA 'NANA'

A magnificent dense and broadly conical or rounded evergreen with glossy dark green leaves that have dramatic orange undersides. Large, deliciously fragrant flowers appear intermittently from midsummer to the early autumn. *M. grandiflora* 'Nana' is denser and more compact than the more widely grown *M. grandiflora*, and so is more suitable for smaller gardens. Thrives in sun or partial shade and fertile, well-drained soil. Height 4.5m (15ft), spread 3m (10ft) after 25 years. Tree.

■ ABOVE
PHORMIUM TENAX 'RAINBOW QUEEN'

Phormiums originally come from New Zealand but despite their exotic appearance are frost hardy. Being evergreen they provide a good "backbone" to the garden and provide colour and interest throughout the year. As the name suggests, this particular plant has a wide range of colours within its sword-like leaves ranging from pink and lemon through orange to bronze. There are bluish-purple flowers in summer, making it one of the most spectacular of phormiums. It requires sun and moist soil and reaches 2–2.5m (7–8ft) in height with a spread of 1m (3ft). Perennial.

■ ABOVE
PRIMULA 'WANDA'

When viewed closely the subtle and varied colour
changes within the leaves of this neat perennial are
quite dramatic. They range from green through
bronze to almost the colour of beetroot at the base.
The wonderful texture of the leaves only serves to
enhance the effect. Come spring and there is a wide
range of flower colours to make for an even more
spectacular effect. Plant in sun or light shade and
keep well-watered. Height 10cm (4in), spread 15cm
(6in). Perennial.

■ ABOVE RIGHT
STIPA ARUNDINACEA

Pheasant grass with clumps of upright evergreen
leaves which start mid-green but become bronzed
and streaked with orangey-red in late summer and
throughout the winter. Graceful drooping panicles
of open, silky, yellowish flowers bloom in summer.
Plant in a well-drained site in full sun. Height 50cm
(20in), spread 90cm (36in). Grass.

■ RIGHT
THUJA OCCIDENTALIS 'ERICOIDES'

A hardy evergreen coniferous tree, slow growing
with dense foliage and a broadly rounded habit. It
has wholly juvenile foliage that is green in summer
turning to walnut brown in autumn and winter. To
obtain the best foliage colour, plant in well-drained
soil in full sun but remember it is easily damaged by
snow. Height and spread 1.2m (4ft). Tree.

Reds

■ ABOVE
ACER PALMATUM DISSECTUM
'CRIMSON QUEEN' AGM

Along with *A. p. d.* 'Red Pygmy' AGM, this is one of the reddest of the Japanese maples, and its foliage turns to a stunning scarlet in autumn. For best results, plant in lime-free soil, sheltered from prevailing winds in light shade. Associates very well with dwarf pines and bamboos to create an atmosphere like that of a Japanese garden. Height 2m (6ft 6in), spread 1.5m (5ft). Tree.

■ ABOVE
ACER PALMATUM 'OSAKAZUKI'

One of the best upright varieties for autumn foliage, rich dark green in summer turning intense crimson in autumn. Cultivation is as for other Japanese maples, remembering this is one of the larger varieties. Generally pest free, like others it may be attacked by aphids which cause sticky and sooty foliage. Height 4–6m (13–20ft). Tree.

■ ABOVE
ACER PALMATUM DISSECTUM
'RED PYGMY' AGM

A tree that is smaller than the average *Acer*. It is slow-growing, reaching its full height only after some 30 years. Some nurseries "cane up" the plants so they reach their final height sooner and fill out accordingly. Plant in lightly shaded acid soil. Height and spread 90–120cm (3–4ft). Tree.

■ RIGHT
BERBERIS THUNBERGII F.
ATROPURPUREA AGM

A rounded deciduous shrub with oval maroon leaves that turn a bright red in autumn. Used as a low hedge it can make an interesting alternative to box. There are no special cultural requirements. Shorten long straggly growth to keep a well-shaped bush. *B.t.* 'Atropurpurea Nana' is a dwarf form 45–60cm (18–24in) high with similar coloured foliage. Height and spread 1.2m (4ft). Shrub.

■ ABOVE
EUONYMUS ALATUS

A slow growing deciduous shrub with an open habit and
curious "wings" to the branches. The narrow oval leaves are
green in summer but turn the most fantastic scarlet in the
autumn. There are small insignificant green-yellow flowers in
summer which are followed by purple fruits with scarlet seeds.
Easily grown in ordinary garden soil in sun or partial shade.
Height and spread 2.4m (8ft). Shrub.

■ ABOVE RIGHT
HEUCHERA 'STORMY SEAS'

Though admittedly it is only the undersides of the leaves that
are red, the contrast with the blue-green upper surface creates
a stunning effect. In addition this pretty plant is fast-growing
and bears white flowers throughout most of the summer. It is
easy to care for, though it should be planted in well-drained
soil and in sun or partial shade. Height 50cm (20in), spread
30cm (12in). Perennial.

■ RIGHT
HOUTTUYNIA CORDATA 'CHAMELEON'

Bog or marginal plant of garden origin, with single white
flowers in summer above the showy, heart-shaped foliage that is
marked with yellow and red, and smells of oranges if crushed.
Although best known as a bog plant it will grow in a surprising
range of conditions but prefers moist, well-mulched soil. Height
30–45cm (12–18in), spread indefinite. Perennial.

■ **LEFT**
IMPERATA CYLINDRICA
'RUBRA'

Japanese blood grass is a hardy upright
grass made all the more startling by the
stark blood-red tips of its pale green leaves.
It associates well with low-growing yellow
or golden-leaved plants. Plant in sun or
partial sun in well-fertilized, moisture-
retentive soil and give some protection
against frost in winter. Remove the seed
heads to prevent self-seeding (and
reversion to plain green). Height 40cm
(16in), spread 30cm (12in). Grass.

■ **BELOW LEFT**
LEUCOTHOE 'ZEBLICH'

This evergreen shrub has leathery, dark
red and green leaves that turn a bright
red in the winter. It has the added bonus
of ornate racemes of white bell-like
flowers that appear in the spring.
Tolerant of shade, it is relatively easy to
care for, though it does best in lime-free
soil. Height and spread 1.2m (4ft). Shrub.

■ **BELOW RIGHT**
NANDINA DOMESTICA AGM

An upright, almost bamboo-like shrub
with pretty, dark green leaves that are a
beautiful crimson colour when young and
in autumn and winter. There are panicles
of white star-shaped flowers in summer
followed by small round berry-like fruits in
autumn, especially if placed in a warm site.
Grow it in fertile, moist, well-drained soil
in a sunny sheltered site. To keep it trim
cut out any old and untidy stems at the
base. Height and spread 1.5m (5ft). Shrub.

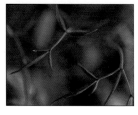

■ ABOVE
PHOTINIA X *FRASERI* 'RED ROBIN' AGM

Although it is just the new leaves that are red, they are such a brilliant red that it is well worth putting up with the dark green that they are for the rest of the year. Broad five-petalled flowers are borne in late spring, which adds to the interest, and it is possible to encourage more red by pruning in the late summer or early autumn. The glossy evergreen leaves are at their best in full sun, and *Photinia* requires fertile, well-drained soil to thrive. Height and spread 6m (20ft). Shrub.

■ ABOVE
PIERIS TAIWANENSIS

Although green for most of the year, this pieris has beautiful coppery-red foliage as well as creamy white flowers in spring. Being a lover of acid soil it teams well with rhododendrons, azaleas and heather. Plant in a shady situation where the foliage will be seen at its best, especially since there is a tendency to scorch in bright sunlight. Avoid chalky or limy soil and keep well watered until established. Height and spread 80–100cm (32–40in). Shrub.

■ RIGHT
SPIRAEA JAPONICA 'MAGIC CARPET'

One of several spireas that have coloured foliage as well as attractive blooms, deep pink in this case. This particular one is enhanced by the new spring growth which is a rich burgundy red and surprisingly frost hardy. Other useful spireas include 'Goldmound', 25cm (10in) high, and 'Goldflame', 60cm (24in) high. All require full sun, moist well-drained soil and a light annual pruning to keep them in shape. Height 45cm (18in), spread 70cm (28in). Shrub.

Purples
and blacks

■ RIGHT

AEONIUM ARBOREUM
'ATROPURPUREUM'

This attractive, purple-leaved form will
revert to green in winter, or if grown in
deep shade in summer. The darkest colour
is achieved in full sun. Because the leaves
are thin, scorching can occur in
midsummer if the plants are too dry. As
the plants soon make new leaves, this is
quickly rectified. Ideal for summer
planting outdoors, but not frost hardy.
Five-years-old pot culture: height 1m (3ft),
spread 60cm (2ft). Succulent.

■ BELOW

AJUGA REPTANS
'BRAUNHERZ' AGM

An evergreen and one of the darkest of the
bugles with its shiny blackish-purple leaves
that are relieved in spring by strong, blue
flower spikes. It makes excellent ground
cover, and provides a striking combination
if planted with miniature narcissus. *A. r.*
'Braunherz' happily tolerates light shade,
but prefers moisture-retentive soil. Height
8cm (3in), spread 40cm (16in). Perennial.

■ RIGHT

ANDROMEDA POLYFOLIA
'COMPACTA'

A delightful and distinctive plant with
small fleshy leaves of both grey and
burgundy forming a well-rounded outline.
Having both these colours, it makes a good
"link" plant to make the transition
between the two colours in the border
more gradual and subtle. Full sun and
good garden soil keep it in top form.
Height and spread 30cm (1ft). Shrub.

■ RIGHT
BERBERIS THUNBERGII 'ROSE GLOW'

Although the mature foliage of this deciduous shrub is a rich deep
burgundy colour it is the bright red of the new growth that makes
this plant spectacular. When nearing its full size there are enough
bright, fresh leaves to make the whole plant really glow – an
appropriate name for a plant if ever there was one. It is useful in a
variety of applications, either as a specimen shrub or an interesting
hedge. Plant in sun or part shade adding plenty of organic matter
to the soil. Height 1.5m (5ft), spread 1.2m (4ft). Shrub.

■ ABOVE AND INSET RIGHT
CANNA HYBRIDS

These exotic-looking plants from the warmer parts of North and South America have
been described as the lazy gardener's delight. They come into bloom early and
continue until the first frost, combining spectacular red, orange or yellow flowers
with interesting foliage. Mostly the leaves are dark bronze or purple-bronze, but
some are brightly variegated. Being frost tender, in temperate climates the rhizomes
need to be lifted and stored frost-free in slightly damp soil or peat during the winter.
Height 1.2–1.8m (4–6ft), spread 0.6m (2ft). Perennial.

■ RIGHT
CIMICIFUGA RACEMOSA

This hardy herbaceous perennial also goes under
the interesting name of black snake-root. It is a
tall graceful plant with wand-like white flowers
that are borne in summer. The fern-like leaves
are attractively veined and on closer inspection
are a rich dark burgundy colour. Plant if the
ground is not frozen or waterlogged during
spring, summer and early autumn, in a lightly-
shaded position in moist leafy soil. Height 1.5m
(5ft), spread 60cm (2ft). Perennial.

■ LEFT
COTINUS COGGYGRIA 'ROYAL
PURPLE' AGM

A deciduous, bushy shrub with dark wine-
coloured leaves that turn red in the
autumn. Tiny flower stalks appear in
midsummer to form pale clusters that look
somewhat like plumes of smoke, an effect
which has given *C. coggygria* its common
name of Smoke tree. It can be planted
singly with a *Choisya ternata* 'Sundance'
for a dramatic colour contrast. It needs full
sun to bring out the best of its colours, and
fertile but not over-rich soil. Height 2.4m
(8ft), spread 2.4m (8ft). Shrub.

■ LEFT AND INSET ABOVE
LOBELIA CARDINALIS AGM

Grown not only for its lance-shaped dark
burgundy leaves but also its brilliant red
flowers which make a stunning
combination with the foliage, *L. cardinalis*
is an excellent clump-forming perennial.
L. 'Queen Victoria' AGM is similar. Both
prefer sun and moist soil, though *L.*
'Queen Victoria' can even be grown in
shallow water, where it can make a striking
edging to a pond. Height 75cm (30in),
spread 30cm (12in). Perennial.

■ RIGHT
OPHIOPOGON PLANISCAPUS 'NIGRESCENS' AGM

There is only one truly black-leaved plant and this evergreen, spreading perennial is the
one. Dramatic, glossy, grass-like leaves slowly spread out to form clumps that show white-
tinged violet flowers in the summer followed by purple-black berries. It is a plant that
creates interest anywhere thanks to its unique foliage. Needs sun or partial shade and fertile,
well-drained soil. Height 15cm (6in), spread 30cm (12in). Perennial.

■ ABOVE

OXALIS TRIANGULARIS SSP. *PAPILIONACEA*

The last part of this tender perennial's Latin name makes reference to butterflies, and when you see a healthy example it really does look as if a cluster of velvet red butterflies has gathered on the ground. There are small pink flowers but these are insignificant compared to the wonderful foliage. Plant outdoors where the average minimum temperature does not fall below -7°C (20°F). Height 10cm (4in), spread indefinite. Perennial.

■ LEFT

PITTOSPORUM TENUIFOLIUM 'PURPEUREUM'

This plant is highly valued as something of a rarity as there are not many evergreen shrubs with purple foliage. The leaves are a very dark and glossy purple and make up a dense bushy shrub. *P. t.* 'Tom Thumb' is similar in form though about half the size, with pale green young leaves and deep reddish-brown older ones. If lightly sheared, they both make excellent hedges. They grow very well in coastal areas, and are at their best in full sun and well-drained soil. Height 1.8m (6ft), spread 1.2m (4ft). Shrub.

■ ABOVE
ROSA 'RUBY WEDDING'

Although renowned for their spectacular
blooms it should not be forgotten that
many roses also have dramatic foliage to
further lengthen their season of interest –
in this case the leaves are a rich deep ruby
colour. The foliage provides a splendid
backdrop for the bright red flowers and
looks superb when the plant is in full
bloom. Like all roses this one requires an
open aspect with rich soil and an annual
dosage of manure. Height and spread 1.2m
(4ft). Shrub.

■ ABOVE
SALVIA OFFICINALIS 'PURPURESCENS' AGM

This purple variety of sage is familiar to many, and can be put to the same culinary uses as the
common variety. Although evergreen, it is not at its best in winter, but it more than makes up
for it in the summer with the bonus of its racemes of lilac-coloured flowers. The matt-felted
foliage contrasts well with plants with glossy leaves such as *Bergenia*. Plant in full sun and in
well-drained soil. Height 60cm (24in), spread 75cm (30in). Shrub.

■ LEFT
SAMBUCUS 'BLACK BEAUTY'

Quite a recent introduction, 'Black Beauty' is an almost-black elder with beautiful, intricately-
shaped leaves. The fragrant creamy-white flowers in early summer are followed by black
fruits. Can look lovely with a climber such as clematis trained through it. Will thrive in sun or
shade, but needs fertile, moist soil. For the best foliage effect, you can cut all shoots to ground
in winter (this will keep the plant small), or just prune out old shoots and reduce the length of
the young ones by half. Height 3m (10ft), spread 2.5m (8ft). Shrub.

Greys and silvers

■ RIGHT
AGAVE AMERICANA AGM

This perennial succulent has sharp, spiky leaves forming a huge basal rosette. Plant in very well-drained soil in a sheltered, warm, sunny location. Because their water requirement is so low they are ideal pot plants and thus can be overwintered indoors; indeed some protection is advisable if left outside during the colder months. Height 1m (3ft), spread 1m (3ft). Perennial.

■ BELOW
ARTEMESIA LUDOVICIANA
'SILVER QUEEN' AGM

Commonly known as wormwood, this bushy perennial spreads to form a thick carpet of deeply cut silver-grey foliage. A similar choice in colour and size would be *A. l.* var. *albula* which has aromatic, silvery-white foliage. Both require full sun and good drainage. Height 60cm (24in), spread 90cm (36in). Perennial.

■ RIGHT
ASTELIA
CHATHAMICA AGM

An eye-catching plant, not unlike a phormium, with its sword-shaped silvery-blue leaves and clump-forming habit. It should be planted in a sunny position in light and well-drained soil. *A. chathamica* should be protected in the winter, although it will re-grow if cut down by frost. Height 1.5m (5ft), spread 1.5m (5ft). Perennial.

■ RIGHT
CALLUNA
VULGARIS
'ALISON YATES'

A heather with long
racemes of white
flowers from
midsummer to late
autumn and silver-grey
leaves. *C. v.* 'Alison
Yates' is a vigorous
plant. Keep it happy by
growing it in acid soil
and keeping well
mulched with peat or
any lime-free peat
substitute. Height
45cm (18in), spread
60cm (24in). Shrub.

■ ABOVE
DUDLEYA BRITTONII

Perhaps the most beautiful of the *Dudleya*
genus with rosettes of broad, white,
powdery leaves. This species is slow to
branch and will normally do so only on old
plants with longish stems. Reasonably easy
to grow, it requires full sun for the best
colour. It is advisable not to handle the
plants too much as the white, waxy farina
on the leaves is easily removed. Minimum
temperature 3°C (37°F). Five-years-old pot
culture: height 10cm (4in), spread 10cm
(4in). Succulent.

■ LEFT
EUCALYPTUS GLAUCESCENS

Also known as the Tingiringi gum, this is
one of the more striking gum trees though
just as versatile as its relatives. Though its
small, round, silvery leaves become longer
and greener as they grow older, the tree
can be stooled annually (cut to the desired
height and allowed to re-grow), which has
the effect of maintaining the silvery foliage.
Grow in full sun and fertile, well-drained
soil, but provide shelter from strong cold
winds. Height 12m (40ft), spread 4.5m
(15ft). Tree.

■ ABOVE
HELICHRYSUM ITALICUM SSP.
SEROTINUM

A dense and rounded shrub with mustard-yellow flowers, fine, narrow leaves that are silvery with a dense felt of white hairs, and a distinctive aroma, which gives it the name Curry plant. This dwarf version is more dense than the more common variety, which makes it particularly useful as an edging plant. To keep its compact shape, give it a light trim after flowering. Needs sun and well-drained soil, and dislikes winter wet and cold climates. Height 60cm (24in), spread 90cm (36in).

■ LEFT
EUPHORBIA HORRIDA

This cactus-like species is quite variable in diameter and colour; the short, swollen, ribbed stems have horizontal stripes in grey-green and silver, and the young spines can be bright red. Attractive but slow-growing , it needs at least 7°C (45°F) in winter when it should be kept completely dry. Five-years-old pot culture: height 7cm (3in), spread 3cm (1in). Succulent.

■ ABOVE
HEUCHERA MICROMINTHA
'PEWTER MOON'

Very useful as ground cover, this is an
attractive plant with marbled pewter-grey
leaves which are a distinctive maroon on
the underside in early summer. The
summer also brings pink flowers on
upright spires. Does better in semi-shade
and moisture-retentive but well-drained
soil. Height 30cm (12in), spread 45cm
(18in). Perennial.

■ RIGHT
LAMIUM MACULATUM 'WHITE
NANCY' AGM

A fine carpeting plant with distinctive
silvery white-green heart-shaped leaves,
that are complemented by clear white
flowers from late spring. It creates a very
interesting contrast of colours when paired
up with *Ophiopogon planiscapus*
'Nigrescens', and brightens up a dark
corner. *L. m.* 'White Nancy' thrives in
shade or partial shade. Plant in moist but
well-drained soil. Height 12cm (5in),
spread 30cm (12in). Perennial.

■ RIGHT
SALIX INTEGRA
'HAKURO-NISHIKI'

A spectacular deciduous ornamental willow with green-and-white blotchy leaves, the young ones being completely pinkish-white. When viewed from a distance, it almost seems to shimmer. Plant against a dark background for best effect. It does not require pruning but if old growth is cut back in early spring the young foliage will be even more dramatic. It can also be grown as a standard. Being a willow it prefers a damp situation and thrives in both sun and partial shade. Height 1m (3ft), spread 1.2m (4ft). Shrub.

■ ABOVE
LAVANDULA ANGUSTIFOLIA
'HIDCOTE' AGM

One of the best-known and most reliable of the lavenders, this bushy evergreen shrub has a compact habit with aromatic silver-grey leaves and with strongly scented violet-blue flowers that appear in the late summer. The plants can be used to form attractive and fragrant low-growing hedges. Plant in full sun and in light, well-drained soil. Height and spread 45cm (18in). Shrub.

■ RIGHT
SANTOLINA
CHAMAECYPARISSUS

One of the palest of all grey plants, looking almost ghostly under a full moon. It has deeply divided aromatic foliage and looks well with other Mediterranean plants. These origins also mean it needs plenty of sun and a free-draining soil. It has bright yellow flowers in summer which may be better removed if the full effect of the grey is to be preserved. Height and spread 50–60cm (18–24in). Shrub.

The Grower's Guide

Buying plants

■ BELOW
A good root system that shows plenty of
growth without the roots being congested.

The majority of plants are sold in
containers at nurseries and garden
centres. Some nurseries specialize in
variegated plants, silver-leaved plants,
or plants with coloured foliage, and
many offer a mail-order service.
Garden centres tend to stock only the
most popular varieties.

The best advice for buying plants
with coloured foliage is to buy them
when you see them. Some
publications list plants and their
suppliers, but not all growers supply
by mail order, and the listing of a
plant does not guarantee its
availability. Further, nurserymen do
not always list all their stock in their
catalogues. This can be because they
know that certain plants are easily
damaged in transit (usually because
they have brittle stems) or because
they cannot produce them in
sufficient quantities to satisfy the
anticipated demand. Some mail-order
nurseries will dispatch a similar plant
if the one you ordered is unavailable,
and it is wise to stipulate whether this
policy is acceptable to you or not
when you place the order. Remember
that you may have to wait a
considerable time for a particularly
rare variety to become available.

It is especially worth buying trees,
conifers and shrubs on sight if they

have been seed-raised, since leaf
colour can vary from one seedling to
the next. Having the full range in
front of you allows you to select the
one with the colour that suits your
scheme best. Buying deciduous trees
and shrubs and herbaceous perennials
when they are in full growth in spring
or summer means you can be sure
you are buying the correct form.

■ BELOW
The roots of this
Carex are very
congested and the
plant is pot-
bound. It will be
difficult to
establish if planted
in the open.

■ BELOW
Nowadays most good nurseries should
have a wide range of coloured foliage
plants in the sales area.

Choosing healthy plants

Look for plants that are healthy and vigorous and show no signs of disease or pest attack. The topgrowth of trees and shrubs should be in proportion to the size of the pot. Even growth is also important: a lop-sided plant will continue to grow lop-sidedly in the garden. Conifers in particular should not have any bare patches.

The presence of a few weed seedlings on the surface of the compost is no cause for concern; if anything, it indicates that the compost is still fertile. If the compost is shrinking away from the pot, the plant has probably not been watered frequently enough. However, moss and lichens on the surface suggest the plant may have been overwatered and is waterlogged.

Where possible, slide the plant from its container to check the roots (they may be just beginning to peep through the drainage holes at the base of the pot). The roots should fill the pot nicely and look healthy. If they are tightly coiled around the inside of the pot, the plant is "pot-bound". The likelihood is that they will continue to grow in a spiral once in the ground, and the plant will be slow to establish or will not establish at all. If they have emerged from the base of the pot, you will have difficulty extracting the plant from the pot, and it should likewise be rejected.

Most reputable nurseries will replace a plant that fails, assuming you planted it correctly, or if the wrong plant is supplied in error.

Cultivation

Before planting, you need to assess the site and soil carefully. Not all plants are adapted to all situations. It is a better policy to choose plants that will thrive in the prevailing conditions than to try to adapt the conditions to satisfy a particular range of plants.

Soil profile

One of the simplest ways to establish soil profile is to pick up a handful and squeeze it in your palm.

If it binds into crumbs that you can rub through your fingers like pastry, leaving your hands clean, you have what is usually termed a friable loam. This is soil that contains a good balance of sand (for drainage) and humus (decayed vegetable remains that hold moisture and hence nutrients). It allows excess moisture to drain through and is easy to dig.

A handful of clay soil forms a solid lump that retains the impression of your fingers. If it fails to bind but trickles through your fingers, the soil is sandy.

A moist but well-drained loam will support the vast majority of plants. However, there are some plants that positively revel in soils that are apparently less than ideal. Nearly all Mediterranean, grey-leaved, woolly

1 Mark out the shape of the flowerbed that you want. For irregular shapes you can use a hosepipe as a guide.

3 After lifting the turf and digging out any remaining roots, add plenty of organic soil conditioner.

2 For a circle, you can tie a piece of string to a post with a sharp stick or tool attached at the other end.

4 Dig the soil over well to break up any heavy lumps and to incorporate the soil conditioner.

and succulent plants do best in a free-draining, nutrient-poor soil. Such soils are quick to warm up in spring and do not freeze in winter. Bog plants, such as *Rheum palmatum* 'Atropurpureum', prefer heavy, sticky ground which does not dry out in summer.

Improving the soil

All soils can be improved by digging in organic matter prior to planting. This helps moisture retention on light, free-draining soils and opens up heavy clay (which you can lighten further by digging in grit).

The best soil improver is garden compost, made by rotting down vegetable matter. Farmyard manure (whether of horses, cows or poultry) is also excellent, but contains fewer nutrients in relation to its bulk. Both must be stacked for a minimum of six months before use, and should only be added to the soil when fully rotted. Poultry manure in particular,

TESTING FOR ACIDITY/ALKALINITY

1 Collect the soil sample from 5–8cm (2–3in) below the soil surface. It is best to take several samples from different beds.

2 Add clean water to the proportion specified. Shake vigorously and then draw off some settled liquid for your test.

3 Add the indicator chemical to the solution. Shake again, and then compare the colour with the shade panel.

which is high in nitrogen, must be thoroughly decomposed, as otherwise it can "burn" the tender new growth of plants.

If you do not have room for a compost heap or have no access to a farm or stable, you can buy proprietary soil improvers based on animal manures at most garden centres, bagged up like potting compost. These have the advantage of being pleasant to handle and are weed-free.

Acid or alkaline?

Acidity and alkalinity are measured in terms of the pH scale, running from 1 to 14. Seven indicates neutral, with lower numbers on the scale being acid, and the higher ones alkaline. Most soils are slightly acid.

The majority of plants are indifferent to a soil's pH. You only need to measure it if you wish to grow certain types of plant. All rhododendrons and camellias and most heathers must have acid soil; clematis, ivies and *Dianthus* prefer alkaline soil (but tolerate some acidity). Some trees and shrubs produce their best autumn colour on acid soil.

You can easily measure the soil pH using a chemical kit, available at garden centres.

Site and aspect

Site and aspect can be critical factors in determining how well a particular plant performs in your garden. Few plants with coloured foliage will do well in deep shade, a notable exception being the spotted laurel (*Aucuba japonica* 'Crotonifolia').

Grey-leaved plants, particularly if hairy or powdery, produce their best colour in full sun. This also applies to thick-leaved plants. Most glaucous plants also need sun, apart from hostas, which are best in shade.

Conifers are best in a sunny and fairly open position, but need shelter from cold, drying winds, particularly when young.

Purple-leaved plants need sun to deepen the colour, and most variegated plants need sun to enhance the variegation.

Trickiest to place are the yellow-leaved plants, which need sun for the best leaf colour (in shade they turn green), but can easily scorch. The ideal site is beneath deciduous trees, where they will receive maximum light in spring, when their leaf colour is at its most intense, but be in dappled shade at the height of summer. Failing such an ideal situation, position them where they will be shaded when the sun is at its hottest (around midday in summer), in the lee of a wall, or near an evergreen shrub, for instance.

Planting

■ BELOW
A circular bed planted with diverse foliage
like this one will provide an oasis of
interest in your lawn throughout the year.

Whatever their individual cultivation requirements, the planting procedure is the same for all plants. Thorough soil preparation prior to planting helps plants establish quickly and cuts down on maintenance later on.

Before planting, dig over the ground and remove all traces of perennial weeds such as bindweed and couch grass. Dig in grit if the soil is heavy and some kind of soil conditioner (see Cultivation) if it is poor.

If you are planting a whole border, or part of a border, set the plants out on the soil surface to determine the best positions. You need to bear in mind the ultimate spread of the plants and space them accordingly. Ideally, at the height of summer plants should just touch at the edges without encroaching on each other, but there is no need to be too precious over this. Most gardeners find they have to thin the planting at some stage, and any awkward gaps in the planting in the short term can be plugged with annuals.

Container-grown plants can be planted at any time of year when the ground is workable – not when waterlogged, frozen or during a prolonged drought. Spring and autumn usually provide the ideal

conditions. Evergreens and plants of borderline hardiness are best planted in spring, which gives them a whole season to establish before their first winter.

On trees and shrubs, cut back any dead, diseased or damaged growth.

■ ABOVE
Even trees that are already established can be transplanted with some care and effort.

You can also shorten the remaining stems, but this is seldom absolutely necessary. Single-stemmed trees should be attached loosely to a short stake that reaches about one-third of the way up the bare length of stem.

Applying a mulch to a new planting prevents evaporation of water from the soil surface, thus cutting down on watering, suppresses weeds and helps feed the soil as it breaks down. However, if the mulch is wet, make sure it does not touch the collar of the plant, since this could lead to rotting.

Mediterranean plants that need hot, dry conditions (and will not tolerate too much wet around their roots) are best top-dressed with grit or small pebbles.

Aftercare

New plantings need regular watering during their first growing season to ensure they establish quickly. Remove weeds regularly, by hand or with a hoe or trowel, in order to keep the area around the base of shrubs, trees and conifers weed free: weeds rob the soil of moisture, which inhibits root growth. Provided you have prepared the soil adequately, supplementary feeding should not be necessary. For further information, see Routine maintenance.

PLANTING A PERENNIAL

1 Dig a hole that is roughly twice the width and depth of the container the plant is in, heaping the excavated soil to one side.

2 Work in organic matter and/or grit at the base of the hole. You can also fork in a little general fertilizer if the soil is nutrient poor.

3 Slide the plant from its container and carefully tease out the roots around the edge. (This will help the roots grow away more quickly.)

4 Set the plant in the hole and check the planting depth with a cane. The compost surface should be at the same level as the surrounding soil.

5 Backfill with the soil that you excavated earlier. Take care not to damage the roots of the plant with the edge of your spade.

6 Firm the plant in. This can be done with your foot though if the soil is heavy and compacts easily, it is better to use your hands.

Growing in containers

Most plants can be grown successfully in containers (with the possible exception of bog plants) provided you adhere to the guidelines below. A huge range of containers is available, and your choice depends largely on your budget, and the type of plant you are growing.

Most containers are suitable for most plants. Try and match the container to the plant, for practical as well as aesthetic reasons. Tall grasses look stylish in tall, elegant pots, but choose a shallow trough or pan for drought-tolerant plants like sempervivums that need only a shallow root run. Very heavy plants such as conifers and evergreen shrubs are best planted in correspondingly heavy containers.

■ LEFT
In this evergreen container, the deep-green leaves and the crimson flower buds of *Skimmia japonica* 'Rubella' contrast strikingly with the brilliant yellow of an *Elaeagnus pungens* 'Maculata'.

Types of container

Terracotta is the traditional material for plant pots, usually in an attractive shade of tan that is sympathetic to nearly all plants. They age beautifully, generally acquiring an attractive patina of salts that leach through them. On the debit side, water evaporates through the sides, making them prone to drying out. They chip easily, and, unless frostproof, can suffer severe damage in a hard winter.

■ ABOVE
It is not advisable to keep plants in their original containers for too long.

Glazed terracotta pots, usually of Far Eastern origin and often sold in matching sets, look good even when empty. They are less likely to dry out than unglazed terracotta. Make sure the colour suits that of the plant you are using.

Light and cheap, plastic pots can be used for all plants. Some are designed to imitate natural materials such as terracotta, stone or lead. Plastic pots are easy to clean and, being water-impermeable, retain water well. However, they can react adversely to direct sunlight which can cause cracking, and they do not usually age well.

Stone and lead containers are extremely expensive and heavy to move, but give style to any setting. Wooden half-barrels are attractive in a rural setting, but their life-span is limited, making them unsuitable for long-term plantings.

PLANTING A CONTAINER

1 After placing some drainage material in the bottom of the container, partly fill it with the appropriate compost.

2 If you like, you can also add some pellets of slow-release fertilizer to the compost to provide a long-lasting supply.

replace up to one-third of the compost with grit. Leaf mould can be added in the same ratio to the compost for woodland plants.

3 Set the plant in the pot and backfill with more compost, leaving a 2.5–5cm (1–2in) gap to allow for watering.

4 Water well throughout the year. The soil in containers dries out much more quickly than that in the open ground.

Aftercare

Do not allow the compost to dry out excessively between waterings. Equally, you need to avoid waterlogging: raising the pot on special feet will allow water to drain freely. You will need to water once and probably twice a day in summer. Water in the evenings, when moisture loss through evaporation will be less.

The fertilizers in the compost will be depleted in six to eight weeks, so feed the plants with a fertilizer formulated for container plants. Fertilizers that are high in potassium promote flower production. A high nitrogen content will encourage leafy growth. Take care not to overfeed, and do not feed after the middle of summer. You can cut down on maintenance by adding water-retaining gel to the compost on planting and by using slow-release fertilizer tablets – some are effective for a whole season. Protect plants in containers from hard frosts in winter by taking them indoors or wrapping them in horticultural fleece.

Composts

Always use proprietary composts, which are sterile and weed-free, rather than garden soil, which contains bacteria and other organisms that can multiply to harmful levels within the confines of a container. If you opt for a soil-based compost (potting mix),

choose one appropriate for standard perennials and grasses, or trees, shrubs and conifers.

Acid-loving plants (most heathers, all rhododendrons and camellias, and some other plants) are best in ericaceous compost, which has the appropriate level of acidity. For drought-tolerant plants, you can

Routine maintenance

Correct planting should ensure that plants grow away without further intervention from the gardener. However, some do need attention from time to time to keep them healthy and to maintain the best display.

Weeding

Keeping your borders free of weeds is very important if your plants are to flourish. Unchecked, the weeds will soon take over and swamp the other plants in a bed.

Perennial weeds, such as couch grass and bindweed, should be removed at planting time (see Planting), but annual weeds will appear in all gardens from seeds deposited by birds or carried by insects. The very act of planting brings dormant weed seeds to the surface, which then germinate.

Remove weed seedlings as soon as you see them. In spring, you can simply hoe them out (the tops can be left on the soil surface – they will rapidly break down over summer) or remove them individually with a hand trowel or hand fork. All annual weeds can be composted, but not if they have already set seed.

Tap-rooted weeds such as dandelions can be difficult to remove.

The best policy if you cannot easily dislodge them is to use a spot weedkiller applied to the leaves. Spot weedkillers can also be used on bindweed and other perennial weeds. Their action is systemic: they enter the plant's system and cause its death without poisoning the soil.

Mulching

Annual mulches of organic matter, applied in spring or autumn, are beneficial to most plants. The mulch helps suppress weeds and also prevents evaporation of moisture from the soil surface. As they break down, they add humus to the soil, greatly increasing the nutrient quotient.

■ ABOVE
The mulch around this hosta will help to retain moisture and suppress weeds.

Garden compost, composted bark, or well-rotted farmyard manure are suitable for most plants. If the mulch is dry, spread it evenly over the soil surface to a depth of 5–10cm (2–4in). If wet, apply it in a donut-like ring around individual plants. Direct contact between a wet mulch and a plant can lead to rotting.

Mediterranean and other plants adapted to poor soil are better if mulched with grit. This has all the benefits of an organic mulch without increasing soil fertility. Grit also reflects sunlight onto the leaves, often enhancing the foliage effect.

A dry mulch around their crowns can protect plants vulnerable to frost such as phormiums. In late autumn, pack dry straw around the base of the plant, keeping it in position with a piece of chicken wire pegged to the soil or weighed down at the edges with stones or bricks. Remove the mulch in spring and cut back any damaged growth.

Watering

Plants should be watered regularly during the first growing season after planting. Water generously, so that the soil is thoroughly irrigated, using a watering can with a fine rose or a

■ LEFT
It is advisable to use a fine rose such as this one on your watering can so as to avoid compacting the earth around the plant.

hose with a sprinkler attachment. Too heavy a jet of water will compact the soil and water will run off the surface rather than filter through. Annuals also need regular watering as do plants in containers.

In subsequent years, supplementary watering of plants in the open garden should not be necessary.

Feeding

Foliage plants should not generally need additional feeding if the soil is kept in good heart by regular mulches of organic matter. Excessive applications of fertilizer can be harmful to plants adapted to poor conditions, such as most of the hairy and woolly-leaved plants. Although fertilizers can give plants a boost, this often results in sappy growth which is vulnerable to disease and cold.

However, a fast-acting foliar feed can help revive a plant that has been set back by a sudden unexpected cold spell or one that is recovering from a pest infestation.

Pruning

Few trees and shrubs actually need regular pruning, but in some cases it can be used to enhance the foliage effect by encouraging new growth.

Catalpas, dogwoods, *Eucalyptus gunnii* and *Cotinus* can all be cut back hard annually in spring to encourage them to produce larger leaves. In the case of the evergreen eucalyptus, this practice stimulates a flush of fresh young leaves, which are coin-like in shape and have a more pronounced bluish-silver cast than the mature leaves, which are sickle-shaped and a dull pewter grey.

Lightly trimming back *Philadelphus coronarius* 'Aureus' just before flowering stimulates a further crop of bright yellow young leaves just as the spring leaves are deepening to green. This is at the expense of the flowers, however.

Apart from yew (*Taxus baccata*), which has an attractive golden form, 'Aurea' conifers do not respond well to pruning.

Watch out for plain green shoots on variegated plants, both deciduous and evergreen. If allowed to develop, they can take over the whole plant, since they are always more vigorous. Cut them back to their point of origin, reaching right into the centre of the bush, if necessary. Golden-leaved forms of privet (e.g. *Ligustrum ovalifolium* 'Aureum') also have a habit of reverting to plain green.

Judicious thinning of some shrubs can be advisable as they mature, to prevent a build-up of old wood (which is less vigorous than young growth and more susceptible to disease) and to lessen the risk of air stagnating in the middle of the bush – ideal conditions for mildew.

Prune deciduous shrubs when dormant in winter, evergreens in spring or midsummer, and cut back shrubby herbs in spring.

TRIMMING A *NEPETA*

1 A *Nepeta* showing dead growth as winter approaches. This has to be removed to ensure good foliage in spring.

2 Remove all of the dead growth using a sharp pair of garden shears. Cut the plant back as far as you can.

3 Ensure however that you do not remove any new growth as you get close to the roots of the plant.

4 Remove any weeds around the plant using a small garden fork, but take care not to damage the root system.

5 Though it seems drastic, this is how the *Nepeta* should look with all the dead growth removed.

6 Carefully top dress the plant with mulch to retain moisture, deter weeds, and provide nourishment for new growth.

Cutting back perennials

While certain perennials die back completely and disappear under ground, others, while not being evergreen, have topgrowth that withers but remains over winter. Many grasses behave in this way.

The dead growth must be cut back annually to allow for the new growth. Whether you do this in spring or autumn is a matter of choice. Tidy gardeners who dislike the sight of dead stems in the gardens over winter cut their perennials down in autumn. They also have the strong argument that decaying plant material in the garden provides a nesting place for overwintering pests such as slugs and snails and can also harbour disease. Other gardeners feel that leaving the dead growth in place over winter provides the resting crown with some protection against frost.

You may choose to remove entirely the dead growth of plants vulnerable to slugs (such as hostas), but leave it on plants of borderline hardiness.

Chop back the dead growth with shears or secateurs. Most plant remains can be composted, but if you know it to be diseased, burn it.

Pests and diseases

Pests and diseases occur in all
gardens, and how you deal with them
is a matter of choice.

Garden centres stock a range of
chemical products that are
formulated to control specific
problems, such as aphids or grey
mould. Some of these are more eco-
friendly than others. If you opt for
chemical control, follow the
manufacturer's instructions to the
letter as to dilution and rates of
application. Many such products are
ready-diluted for immediate use,
usually as a spray. Dispose of any
excess chemicals safely.

Nowadays, many gardeners prefer
to keep their use of such products to

■ ABOVE
**Aphids can seriously blight otherwise
healthy plants.**

the absolute minimum and adopt a
live and let live policy in the garden.
This is most successful if you grow as
wide a range of plants as possible in
order to create the most diverse eco-
system. Pests will still appear in the
garden, but so will their predators.

The definition of a pest is in any
case open to interpretation.
Caterpillars eat young leaves, but are
an ornament to the garden once they
metamorphose into butterflies. Birds
peck at the unopened buds of trees
and shrubs but also feed on slugs and
snails. Earwigs damage many plants,
but help control aphid populations.

Diseases often strike as the result
of inappropriate cultivation. A plant
in the wrong place will be weak-

growing and vulnerable. Pest damage
will weaken its resources still further,
allowing viruses (some carried by
insects) and fungi to take a hold.

The best way to keep them at bay
is by practising good garden hygiene.
Regularly remove dead or decaying
plant material from around the base
of plants. Sweep up leaves from
deciduous trees and shrubs in
autumn. Prune congested shrubs and
wall climbers in summer to prevent
stagnant air from developing around
the stems.

Heavily diseased plants should be
dug up and burnt. Do not compost
them, since fungal spores can persist
in the compost and be returned to the
soil to affect more plants.

Calendar

■ BELOW
A *Corylus maxima* 'purpurea' next to a
Laburnum in summer.

Early spring

When conditions permit, i.e. the soil is not frozen or waterlogged, plant into containers or ground that has been thoroughly dug over, all weeds removed and well rotted manure or garden compost dug in. Feed and mulch established plants and repot or top dress those in containers with a suitable potting compost. Lightly prune or shape any wayward shrubs such as yew and santolina. Groom any grasses to remove dead foliage.

Start to take cuttings of any suitable shrubs and begin sowing hardy plants under glass.

Late spring

Later in the season hardy plants can be sown direct into the ground. Keep all containers well watered as well as newly planted specimens. Plant cannas and dahlias with coloured foliage such as 'Bishop of Llandaff' once the danger of frost has passed.

Early summer

Continue diligently watering those plants that are in containers. Water may well be required daily and it is worth using a liquid feed every week unless a slow-release fertilizer was used at planting time. Dead-head flowers regularly unless the seed is needed. Continue to take cuttings of favourite plants. Start planning for next year on the basis of how things are shaping up now.

Late summer

As the season progresses gaps may appear in borders as plants die off or are trimmed back. Temporary plants such as coleus or silver-leaved

■ LEFT
An autumn border with *Verbascum* that
has stopped flowering. Fallen leaves will
add their own unique colour to beds.

back. Alternatively, leave dead stems
to protect crowns from frost and
provide sanctuary for overwintering
ladybirds. Mix gravel into areas of
heavy soil to improve drainage over
the winter. Mulch bushy herbs with
gravel to keep their necks dry.

Winter

Continue tidying up the garden when
conditions permit, by dead-heading
and removing dead foliage that may
harbour pests and diseases. Some
winter foliage though can be very
attractive, especially with a covering
of frost. Dig over new borders so the
frost can break up the soil.

cineraria can be used to replace them.
Continue watering as usual, but if the
ground has become very dry, soak the
roots well by using a hose, without a
spray, at ground level.

Mid- and late autumn

Cut herbaceous herbs down to a
crown once their stems have died

Autumn

It is a good time for planting as the
soil is still warm and the rainfall is
higher than in summer. Container-
grown plants can be put in at the
beginning of the season, and bare-
rooted ones later on. Continue dead-
heading and protect tender plants
from frosts. Take hardwood cuttings.
Remove dead foliage from established
plants and mulch with well rotted
manure or garden compost. Divide
any congested perennials.

■ LEFT
A late autumn
border dominated
by the striking red
foliage of *Cornus
alba* 'Sibirica' and
with *Bergenia*
'Sunningdale' in
the foreground.

Other recommended plants

Actinidia kolomikta

Aegopodium podagraria
'Variegatum'

Catalpa bignonioides 'Aurea'

Corylus maxima 'Purpurea'

Actinidia kolomikta
A slender deciduous climber suitable for a sunny and sheltered wall or fence. The foliage is stunning with each green leaf splashed with white or pink at the tip. White flowers are borne in early summer. Plant in rich, well-drained loamy soil. Height 1.8–3.6m (6–12ft).

Aegopodium podagraria
'Variegatum'
This ground-cover plant, with fresh green leaves unevenly edged with creamy white, is a variety of the common ground elder although not quite as rampant in its habit. Plant with equally vigorous plants or confine it to a pot. It does especially well in moist shade. Height 25cm (10in), spread 45cm (18in).

Bergenia 'Bressingham Ruby'
Most of the bergenias have rounded, glossy green leaves

but this one is especially colourful and particularly so in autumn and winter. Does well in sun or light shade as long as the soil is fertile and moist. Height 30cm (12in), spread 45cm (18in).

Canna 'Durban'
Many of the cannas have coloured foliage but this one is particularly spectacular and deserves special mention. The leaves are striped with a whole range of colours including red, yellow, green and brown. Lift and store in a frost-free place during the winter. Height 90cm (3ft), spread 60cm (2ft).

Catalpa bignonioides 'Aurea'
(**Indian bean tree**)
A striking deciduous tree with large gold-coloured, heart-shaped leaves that can be made still larger by annual pruning of the branches in early spring. Thrives best in a

warm sheltered position. Height and spread 4.5–6m (15–20ft).

Cerastium tomentosum
Commonly known as snow-in-summer, this is a useful ground-cover plant with silver-grey leaves and cheery white flowers. It needs a dry, sunny position and benefits from an annual trim. Height 8cm (3in), spread indefinite.

Clematis montana 'Tetrarose'
This variety of *Clematis montana* not only has a mass of pink flowers in spring but also dark and dramatic burgundy-coloured foliage. Plant against a wall or fence, with wires or trellis for support, and shade the roots. Height 12m (40ft), spread 6m (20ft).

Cordyline australis
'Atropurpurea'
This bronze-purple cabbage palm is not quite as hardy as

the green type so needs to be grown in a sunny sheltered position and protected against frosts. Height 9m (30ft), spread 6m (20ft).

Corylus maxima 'Purpurea'
A robust and hardy deciduous shrub with dark purple leaves and catkins that are 7–10cm (3–4in) long followed by oval nuts. Plant in well-drained soil, and in an open site, though it can tolerate partial shade. Height and spread 3m (10ft).

Cupressus macrocarpa
'Goldcrest'
One of the most attractive of the large conifers that boasts pine-scented, feathery foliage. It makes a fine specimen tree and can also be used to form a tall screening hedge. It should be planted in well-drained soil in an open aspect. Height 9m (30ft), spread 2.4m (8ft).

Hebe ochracea 'James Stirling'

Hosta 'Sum and Substance'

Hypericum × *moserianum* 'Tricolor'

Iresine herbstii 'Brilliantissima'

Cynara cardunculus
The cardoon is a much larger relative of the artichoke with huge silvery leaves that can grow up to 1.2m (4ft) long. There are also 2.4m (8ft) long stalks with thistle-like flowers. Plant in good garden soil in full sun. Height 1.8m (6ft), spread 1.2m (4ft).

Euphorbia griffithii 'Dixter'
It is actually the bracts of this plant that are the brightest orange. The olive-green foliage is also tinged with orange. A stunning plant for a "hot" colour scheme in full sun. Height 75cm (30in), spread 60cm (24in).

Fallopia x bohemica 'Spectabilis'
A strikingly beautiful plant. Its tall stems, which later branch, are clothed with leaves about 15cm (6in) long that are irregularly marbled yellow, cream and green.

Grow in light shade to prevent scorching. Height 2.4m (8ft), spread 1.8m (6ft).

Geranium Crug strain
Although quite small this is certainly a plant that stands out. It has bright red leaves that once seen are never forgotten. Like most hardy geraniums it is relatively unfussy in its requirements as long as it is in a light position in good garden soil. Height and spread 15cm (6in).

Hebe ochracea 'James Stirling'
Plants of any description are very rare in this colour, which makes this compact evergreen little shrub especially useful and desirable. The evergreen foliage is a bronzy olive-green colour that has to be seen to be fully appreciated. Plant in full sun to retain the best colour. Height and spread 50cm (20in).

Hemerocallis fulva 'Kwanzo Variegata'
Thin pale green lines run through the centres of the extraordinarily white leaves of this vigorous perennial. When planted in a group next to dark-leaved plants, the effect can be stunning. Light shade and moist, fertile soil are the ideal growing conditions. Height and spread 45cm (18in).

Hosta 'Big Daddy'
This is one of the larger hostas with large, puckered, intensely blue foliage. There are mauve flowers borne in late summer. Like most hostas, it thrives best in moist soil with light shade. Height and spread 75–80cm (30–32in).

Hosta 'Sum and Substance'
Another large hosta, with big golden-yellow leaves that are thick, tough and pest

resistant. Lavender flowers are borne in late summer. Grow in deep, moist, fertile soil in light shade. Height and spread 75cm (30in).

Hypericum × moserianum 'Tricolor'
A stunning variety of the well-known St John's wort. As well as the bright yellow flowers on low-arching stems, it has leaves with a wonderful combination of pale green, cream and reddish pink. Grown in a sunny position in fertile soil, it makes good ground cover although it is not as vigorous as the green-leaved variety. Height and spread 60cm (24in).

Iresine herbstii 'Brilliantissima'
A tender bedding plant best massed in large groups where its bright red leaves and dense habit will help to smother weeds. An interesting effect

Ornamental cabbage 'Fiesta'

Melissa officinalis 'Aurea'

Rosa glauca

Solenostemon scutellarioides

can be had by contrasting it with grey- or silver-leaved plants. Treat like a pelargonium and take cuttings for overwintering. Likes full sun. Height and spread 30–45cm (12–18in).

Libertia perigrinans
Given moist soil and a sheltered, sunny position, this grass-like perennial will reward with startling bright-orange, strap-like leaves. Full sun is essential, otherwise the leaves will begin to revert to green. *Libertia ixioides*, another, smaller variety, has dark-green leaves that turn orange-brown in winter. Height 40cm (16in), spread 20cm (8in).

Melissa officinalis 'Aurea'
This is a variety of lemon balm, which has bright-green leaves attractively speckled with gold. The leaves also have a delightful lemon fragrance. Grow in sun or

light shade. Height and spread 45cm (18in).
Ornamental cabbage
A round-headed cabbage with crinkly leaves that are variegated pink and white. The seeds are usually bought as a mixture. Useful as a filler while young shrubs and perennials are becoming established or as a focal point in their own right, especially over winter when colour can be scarce. Plant in full sun. Height and spread 45cm (18in).

Philadelphus coronarius '**Aureus**'
Deciduous shrub with white cup-shaped flowers that open in summer. They have the most delicious fragrance, reminiscent of orange blossom. The foliage is bright yellow when young, but it becomes greener through the summer as it ages. It retains its colour best

in light shade. Height and spread 1.8m (6ft).
Prunus cerasifera '**Nigra**'
A bushy deciduous tree with a rounded head of black-purple leaves and pink flowers that are borne in spring. Can be used very effectively as hedging in an open aspect in any good garden soil. Height and spread 4.5–6m (15–20ft).
Pyrus salicifolia '**Pendula**'
A delightful deciduous tree with soft grey-green foliage, which would make a striking centrepiece in any garden. It can be lightly trimmed to keep an attractive rounded shape. Requires full sun and well-drained soil. Height and spread 4.5–6m (15–20ft).
Rheum palmatum var. *tanguticum*
A spectacular member of the rhubarb family, especially in the spring when the new growth emerges bright red. Makes a very good focal point

with its large palmate leaves tinged with purple on both sides. Does best in moist soil. Height and spread 1.5–1.8m (5–6ft).
Rosa glauca
A variety of rose with small, delicate, single, pink flowers and unusual grey foliage diffused with a dusky pink. With long arching branches, it makes a striking plant when grown in full sun in well-drained fertile soil. Can be used as a hedge. Height 1.8m (6ft), spread 1.5m (5ft).
Solenostemon scutellarioides
Better known as coleus, these tender perennials sport a huge variety of colour, which can be used to great effect in the foliage border. The colours range over red, yellow, purple, brown and creamy white. Plant in full sun and keep frost-free over winter or treat as annuals. Height and spread 45cm (18in).

Index

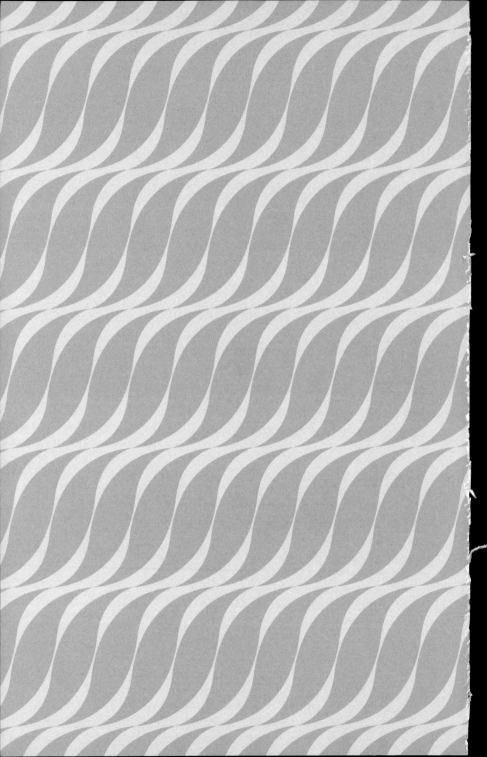